I want to start off by telling you about this book and where these writings came from. Let me tell you a little bit about me and my struggle, so that you and I can relate , so you understand that everyone has suffered, whether it be addictions, past traumas or bad circumstances . Hopefully by the end of this you will realize that no matter what you are currently suffering from, you can find freedom.

Let me take you back to my childhood and adolescence, since most of our emotional baggage comes from this time. I had a normal childhood, I grew up with both parents who worked hard while providing everything I needed. It wasn't until I was about 12 years old or so that I experienced trauma that began to mold my ego. I was molested by this male, which left me feeling afraid, confused and insignificant. After this I had to build this tough, but witty kid who had all the answers. By the time I left middle school I had a monstrous ego that was building an emotional wall, keeping all my healthy loving emotions imprisoned, while not letting anyone too close. You know the feeling, keeping people at arms length, not allowing them to hurt you. In high school I portrayed this rebellious teen, drinking, smoking and selling drugs, so that I could I hide this scared little boy. As I got older I carried this rebellious façade into adulthood, partying all night poisoning my body and destroying the people that love me . I was living an immoral life in my early 20's, as if this wasn't enough chaos. I decided to get married have a couple of kids that I was incapable and selfishly, not able to support or be present for. My mind and actions were that of a very immature boy, this led to many years of guilt, shame and inner turmoil. When all this came crashing down I was forced to look at my life as failing, and I would have to suffer consequences greater than ever before. I would be heading to prison for 5 years. Although, this seemed like the end for me, it was only the beginning. I showed up to prison battered, broken and confused, but I'm not kidding with you when I say... Prison saved my life, but I'll finish that story at the end of this book.

These writings are a reflection of me barely holding on to my grip of reality, I was drowning in a sea of drugs, pity and sorrow, gasping for air when I could. My head and breath were so shallow. I was defeated, demoralized and abused. Life for me was just an vicious cycle of turmoil, sadness and a cry for help. I wrote when I was high, so I wouldn't take my own life. In some of these writings you'll read that I was desperately clinging to life, because I was. The truth is, I had already tried to take my life several times, but something didn't let me. I wrote this book because although I was drowning, there was always a glimmer of hope. Not in my situation, but in me. These writings reflect that.

The main reason I put these writings together is to show you there is hope, life can be wonderful for you as long as you keep trying. Failures are necessary in life, they show us that life is not one-sided, it's hard, even cruel sometimes, but if you make an effort you can endure. You can put your life back together, but it has to be you. The greatest lesson I learned and the reason you're reading this book is because I learned that I was responsible for my happiness and peace. No person, place or thing was responsible for me. I know it might be tough right now, you may be suffering or watching someone you love suffer, but if you read these writings, you will be able to relate and when you get done understanding that we all suffer. I'm going to explain to you how to live life without abusing yourself or those around you, so you can take your life back.

Many blessings

Let Us Pray

My King,

If I am not a slave, then why do shackles of my past still bruise me. I cannot control my own mind, my emotions run wild...remorse has become my best friend. In life all I ask, is freedom. Freedom from my sins of yesterday...amnesty from the wrongs I've done to you and my loved ones. My King, clear my conscious, mark me as a soldier of fortitude and grant me strength to change who I was and shape who I am about to become.

With great respect,

Amen

My King,

My dreams of a new kingdom are being tested, the fear of failure has me distraught, corrupting my peace and willingness. Today, save me from my own demise... Encourage my talents and effort to become who I am meant to be. Allow my own heroism to rise, so that others will find courage to dream, develop bravery and learn from there own omissions...might they find serenity where they only knew conflict.

Amen

Success & Growth is not an option...
I will never surrender to failure.
Excuses & Self Pity are dead.
Progress keeps me alive.
Spirituality & Faith are a must...
I refuse to be common.

FAR

Adonai,

Today help me see past the scrutiny of others, help me understand that though your word lives in me, I'm imperfect. Help me throughout my days with procrastination, for I too allow my days to slip away, leaving only wonder to what I should have been doing. Demonstrate your power and consideration for me, so that I may be considerate of others, not only myself, because in my action of caring there's hope. I don't mean to dismiss others, close my feelings or my mind, but even my defects get the best of me. A wise woman once told me "don't allow your arrogance to roam freely without restraint, for it will hinder relationships that may empower you". Lord, I know I must be considerate of your people, I know that waiting makes me vulnerable to time, so I must keep pushing ahead. Give me drive, action and the initiative to move forward without fear of what the day may bring. I Thank you for your love and kind words.

Amen

Father,

Today is a day of recognition, yesterday my spirit was abandon, I began to feel lonely and unworthy of blessings to come. On my knees last night, I asked why me? The universe owes me nothing. Who will listen to me?
As the morning sun rose,
so did my confidence and spirit anew. Today I will not question your restoration,
I will only obey. Just as Rome was not built in a day, nor will my spirituality. It takes practice, conditioning and trust.
I must have faith in the process, endure the journey and fight through the struggles; for it is easy to trust in serene times.
It's through the hard times where faith diminishes. Father, grant me resilience and nourishment in my time of need, allow me to thrive when some may give up.
For us, I always pray.

Amen

Lord Almighty,

Forgive me my arrogance, my ignorance...
the blasphemy.
Forgive me because sometimes this world fogs my
vision and the wrong seems right it's as though
darkness has engulfed me.
I'm beyond finding the light. Lord don't let me fall
into enemy hands, protect me as I walk beside
you... I am prudent if I am with you, but foolish if I
deny you. This hour I ask for mercy,
crowd me with grace. Grant me dominion over my
feelings and character this day,
give me peace only you can provide, shower me in
love, so that I may illuminate your power and
amplify your voice.
Today and always...I pray.

Amen

Today let me remind you that your pain, your suffering and stress don't go unnoticed. Sometimes we get so broken and mangled We get so bruised and battered that life seems unbearable, almost not worth living. We try keeping our morals intact while fighting a disease that won't let us breath. When I come to the surface I feel myself gasping and choking clinging to my last little bit of hope. This time is going to be different, this time I have a solid foundation and I don't need outside help. The thing is we all need help sometimes, whether help manifests in spirit, friends or institutions we must have the courage to except it.
Jesus said "You are Peter, and upon you I will build my church and not even the gates of Hades will prevail(Matthew 16:18)". Peter which means rock, wasn't just a name or man... He was a solid foundation which Jesus trusted to withstand anything and that nothing would shake peters foundation, and that's YOU.
You are Peter.

Our paths are not always clear or without ruin or obsticles, but day by day we overcome one step at a time. Many times we question the journey, but always have faith in your destination

TRUhope

My Lord,

Thank you for guiding and comforting me when I was lost and alone. Thank you for allowing me to keep my serenity in times of chaos and turmoil. I thank you for sanity through commotion and unwanted past notions, disillusion and disarray. In you Lord I find strength, willpower, justice and courage to fight the demons I once had...protect me Almighty, keep me safe as I journey through this place.

Amen

My Creator,

In this pitch black world my eyes get cloudy, it's hard to focus sometimes, I need only to adjust but instead many times I close my eyes, cower and give up because I'm afraid. I read your words and find hope, but even then it seems as though I am the only one to have faith, this makes me question, Am I alone? When everyone around me lives in the shadows of society, slipping between the cracks, living in poverty, hopelessness and false idolatry...worshiping darkness. I look for you Lord. How do I use your words as guidance? I know through the darkness your path offers happiness and freedom from confinement and false reality, yet It's so difficult to see. I don't want to be lost...please find me, I pray there are no boundaries, no segregation...no darkness. Bestow a torch bright enough to illuminate my path and theirs, so that we may find our way together, so I'm not alone...Lord.
We are afraid to be alone.

Amen

When Jesus spoke again to the people, he said, "I am the light of the world. Whoever follows me will never walk in darkness, but will have the light of life." (John 8:12 NIV)

There is no honor in victory without failure.
When our weaknesses are exposed, only
then is our true strength revealed and
only when we are captive
Will we fight for absolute
Freedom.

Almighty,

I thank you for this day, I pray you hear me,
that I am seen, felt with faith tangible, because
of your presence. Keep my mind grounded in
the present, let me forget tomorrow and
surrender my past. There is no life without love
and there is no love without conquering strife,
compromise or trust. I cannot be in love until I
fully embrace this moment, until I can love
unconditional as you do.
In love, with tolerance I pray.

Amen

Lord,

Why am I so greedy? Why am I so selfish? I don't know why I am depressed, why I seclude myself from the world. I'd rather sit in my own misery, watch clouds of remorse float on by than to apologize or forgive. Why I do this baffles me, this isn't me.
Lord, take my anxiety, take my life. Make me content with the things I have, not to lust over possessions that will fade away. Please help me not destroy me Lord. Show me friends who love sincerely, and hold true to their meaning, not ones who use and abuse. Show me beauty where there is ugliness, shine light on me where there is darkness and give me wisdom before I crumble, stumble or ramble.....please show me.

Amen

My path may be short and serine, yours may be long and treacherous, and although the distance may seem so far and unforgiving...the time and destination are the same...we are the same, just different experiences on our journey.

FAR

My Savior,

Why do I feel lost, alone and abandoned? Am I not to understand my own battle within? Am I so far from the truth that confusion and delusion haunt me? Am I a ghost of the past seeking revenge or justification?

No... I am not alone in this struggle. Not only is my addiction chasing me, but my demons follow suit.

Do I wait for answers? The universe tries my patience, my decisions along with my sickness. My struggles call for answers and attention, but only despair arises. Only when my mind clears do I realize that recovery is a process. The journey is the best part, if only I could focus. I lose sight of the destination so quickly. It's as though I cannot agree with life, keep Love or make sacrifices.

Please give me the strength to show those who do not understand, those who do not see my struggle. We can't be alone.

My savior give me insight, love me always, allow me to endure and I will always trust in you.

Amen

Father,

How long are we willing to suffer for one mistake? Though I have been tried & found guilty by a justice system that's less honorable, faulty men claim jurisdiction over meek men with priors because the past creates fear. I am responsible for my actions, but neither judge, jury or "state" can convict me internally. For my body may be confined, but my heart, spirit and mind are free.
Father, show them that no amount of chains, concrete, or steel can hold me captive. As long as I have a voice or pen I will not be silenced, not by him, them or they. Forgiveness is for me, not for them.

Amen

Keep Faith,

As we are surrounded by chaos and confusion our morals may get disoriented but we pray. I pray for patience and serenity. We don't have to succumb to the craziness that deceives us. Great lessons come from memorable punishment, whether we are misguided or at fault, we overcome by keeping faith. Although it feels punishments are endless and suffering is inevitable, I tell you from experience nothing is permanent.

Everything changes.

Lord,

Help me speak the truth even if it bares momentary pain, unspoken words can wound severely. The hurt from lies only invokes resentment and guilt. There is already so much wreckage caused by past deceit. Lord, heal those who have been hurt by bitter lies and help them recognize I'm just a mortal man. My past intentions are not a reflection of who I really am. Give faith where its needed, I meant no harm, no malice, nor sorrow. Give me the courage to be truthful in all that I do, with whomever I love.

Amen

Ephesians 4:10... Speak the truth in love.

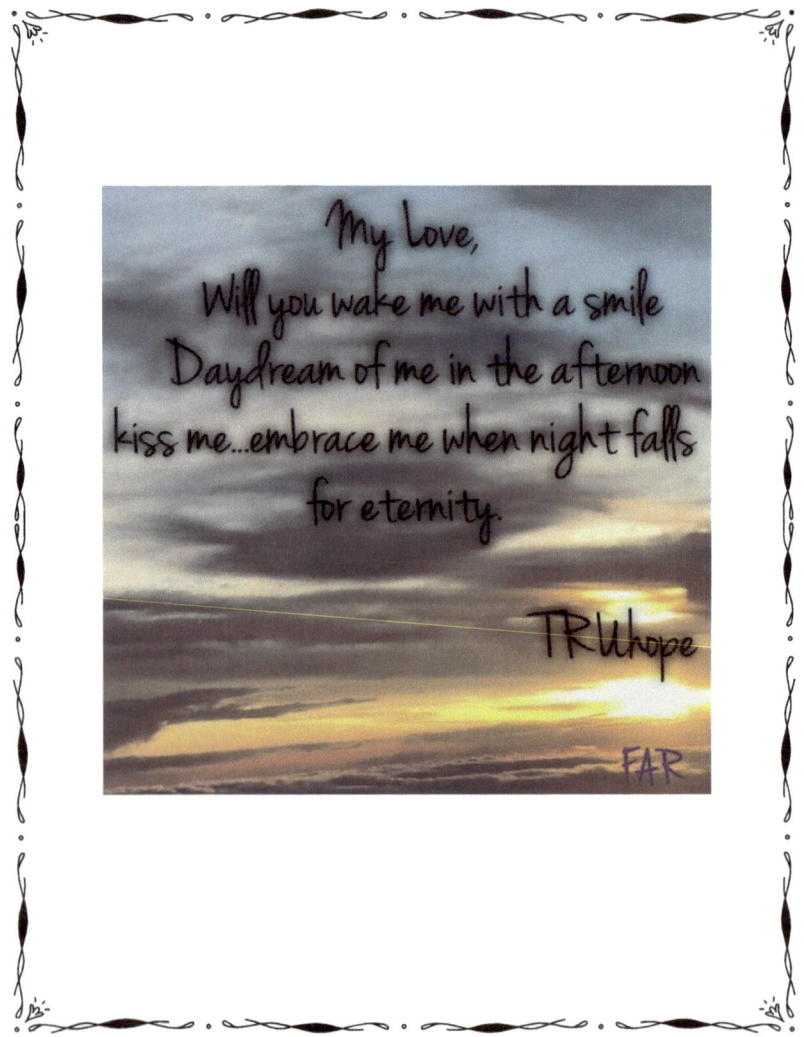

For my children,

I've committed a sin against my children, not only was I absent but neglectful. I was selfishly irresponsible, distant, unreliable, and immature...a shallow father, a shell of a man who was afraid of commitment.
Father, history shall not repeat itself, for you teach me love and forgiveness. Even through guilt and shame there is always hope and revival. Help me mend what was broken, remember what was forgotten. Age does not come without some wisdom, nor mistakes without consequences. My faults do not exclude redemption. Grant me fatherly compassion, sacrifice and understanding to love my children as you love me.

Amen

John 3:16 God loved the world. He gave his only son, so that whoever believed in Him will have eternal life.

Father may I ask you a question?

Father, if my body and mind are free of addiction, then why do I still feel captive by pride, greed and fallacy of complete restoration? Am I to be resurrected with you even though my spirit is in bondage by my flesh? Paul told the Romans not to fear bondage, for your spirit was with them... Is your spirit with me? I am a selfish heathen, Father I sin even when I don't want to...Please help me, make me incorruptible, grant me immortality! Please guide me away from the shadows of my past and into the light of righteousness. I don't want the choice to return to my former life. Can you take the power of choice from me?
Father, am I asking too much?

Amen

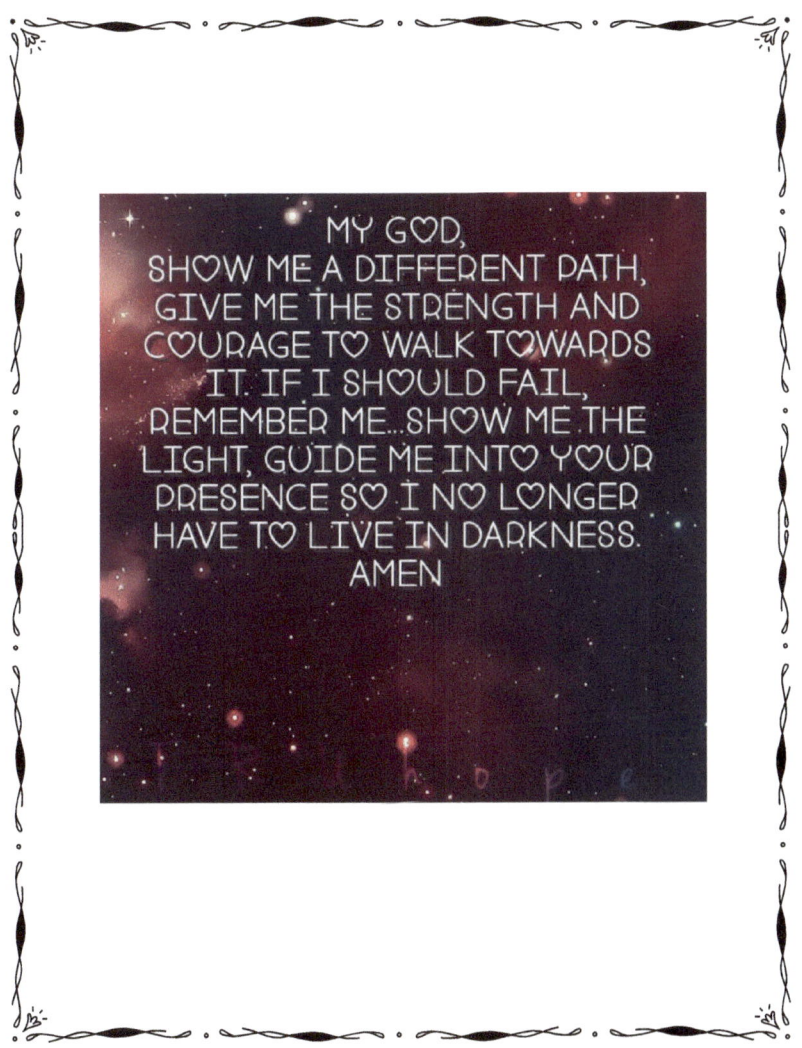

MY GOD,
SHOW ME A DIFFERENT PATH,
GIVE ME THE STRENGTH AND
COURAGE TO WALK TOWARDS
IT. IF I SHOULD FAIL,
REMEMBER ME...SHOW ME THE
LIGHT, GUIDE ME INTO YOUR
PRESENCE SO I NO LONGER
HAVE TO LIVE IN DARKNESS.
AMEN

Lord,

Today, I choose to love life's process, not fear. My failures and faults of yesterday are forgiven and forgotten. Grant me strength to move-on, so I can grow...flourish and breakthrough. Practicing what we love everyday makes permanence, not selfishness. To be present is our accomplishment, with presence we cannot see or truly appreciate the world around us. Give my life meaning, prominence and power today, so that I may shine, as all of us are meant to do.

Amen

Lord,

Today I'm struggling, today I am losing....
Losing my friends, my job, my house, my status....
maybe even my mind.
Give me strength that's all I ask today...help me appreciate
life at its best, and at its worst.
I forget that I'm not worthy is this worlds eyes, but I know
that I matter in yours.
Sometimes we lose to gain, and struggle to win, But I know I
am not a loser.
I am not afraid, and I will not lie down with failure.
I will not cry.
I will stand.
I will fight.
I will overcome.

Thank you for this day.
Amen

Keep hold of what you love.
Be truthful to what you respect.
Appreciate those who believe in you.
Stand by your beliefs & values
because they define you.
Have faith in the dream you chase
& never settle for less.
Be greater than your
circumstances.

FAR

When we are weak, trapped and vulnerable, a strong will is forged. This is not by fear, but by overcoming, by keeping an open mind and understanding we all fear.
When there is nothing to lose, the fear of loss has no power.
Strength is gained through humility and those who know their enemy do not underestimate the power of forgiveness.
It takes guts to fight and endure, but it's wiser to avoid conflict, it expends energy to be angry, argue and cause injury.
It takes patience to outthink those who hurt you and those who hurt you are just afraid.
Destroy your fears,
not each other.

Jesus,

Today I don't want to give up, I want to stand up.
I want to face the day with a loving heart and an
open mind.
If my enemy is scorn let their heart be touched, let
your presence overwhelm their hate, control my
temper, let me hold my tongue.
Help me when my patience wears thin, my wallet
seems thin and my stress seems everlasting.
These things of today are temporary, but your love
is eternal. Help me understand this today.
I am a human with an ugly past that shadows me,
but my soul is pure and innocent, forgive me my
transgressions because I am not perfect.
I follow my heart, close my eyes and hope and pray
for change, for renewal.
This is what I pray for today, yesterday and always.

Amen

Master your journey, so that you can LIVE your destiny

Light of the world,

Make me shine beyond what my eyes can see.
Today I will not collapse, I will not be defeated...no,
not me.
I will not relapse to past failures, nor will I repeat
bad relationships, actions or situations.
The bridges I have built will not crumble beneath
me, my heart is reinforced, strong, willing and
unbreakable.
My skin is thicker, my blood is richer and my
strength is incomparable.
My faith is unmeasurable, my mind is
inconceivable and your miracles are unbelievable.
What a wonderful day.

Amen

Dear materialism,

Why must I work all day to feed my addictions. Has money become my idol?
This world gives me limits on chasing dreams and reaching goals because of prosperity.
I am judged by what I own and not for who I am or what I believe.
My heart is made of gold, but you will never know and no amount of riches will replenish my soul. Yet, I still labor, I am tormented, coaxed, entrapped by eager sentiments brought to life by self indulgence and greed.
How much is enough? I won't let you rule my life, I refuse to have limits on principles, morals or integrity. I will not be a slave.
My potential will not be captive, you're not entitled to my life, nor my tranquility, and though you may deceive and delude the world around me.
I know you're fake, smoke and mirrors, a delusion of temporary happiness.

Sincerely,
FAR

THE ONLY REAL PRISON THAT WILL HOLD YOU CAPTIVE FROM LIFE ... IS A CLOSED MIND

Dear ME,

How are you? Remember the past? We had fun didn't we?
Causing ruckus, running amuck without fear,
obligation...responsibility.
It's time to change, but I wanted to thank you for what you
taught me.
I was brave, adventurous and free-spirited. You gave me
ambition to walk away.
Change isn't easy, I once thought that only the weather
changed but I now know this isn't True.
I'm just not the person we set out to be. Somewhere
between the chaos, confusion and living without purpose. I
figured it out, this life is too short to be selfish, unloving,
miserable and unforgiving.
Our past has come and gone and I'm grateful, but now I
have to prepare for the future.
So, I remember you. I honor you and I'll never forget you.
Heartbreak and heartache are never easy, leaving one life
to another always leaves a scar, but I finally understand.
My scars show ME there is always something
worth fighting for.

Love,
ME

Father,

Today let me forget yesterday, the trails
of the past are gone and today is a
new day.
Let me live in your glory and joy, allow
my heart to express love and kindness.
Allow my mind to be still when needed
and my heart to soften to except help
when needed.
I will worry about the future tomorrow
and thereafter, but today make me
peacefully humble.

Amen

Maker of heaven and earth, Today let me shine on this world, help me reflect on today's issues, not dwell in the negative but stand up for what's right. Today I choose to be happy....today, like every other day is worth living...keep me strong, spiritual and allow my integrity to show.

Ephesians 4:10... Speak the truth in love.

Lord,

Help me speak the truth even if it bares pain
momentarily, unspoken words can wound severely.
The hurt from lies only invokes
resentment and guilt.
There is already, so much wreckage caused
by my past deceit.
Lord, heal those who have been hurt by bitter lies and
help them recognize all truths will reflect their own
intentions, but faith will prevail
through unintentional sorrow.
Strength comes from pain,
there is so much pain lord.
Give me the courage to be truthful in all that I do, with
whomever I love.

Amen

God,

Grant me the strength to push my emotions aside, to live through today's struggles without fear or damnation.
Please help me if I fall, fail or stumble. Guide me if I'm led astray.
Thank you for amplifying your voice, because sometimes I'm deaf, broken and lonesome.
Thank you for silence, so that I may hear your voice even through the noise around me. Heal my mind, spirit and body today.
I bow to you Lord and only you.

Amen

For those who are losing faith,

Faith cannot be lost.
We can lose people, friends and time, but
faith is everlasting.
Jesus had Faith till death, but he knew even after
death there was life, liberty and unconditional love.
We sometimes forget we have blemishes, no matter
how pure the heart, there are always flaws. Forgive
me my weakness, my inadequacy, my lack of love
and failures. I am human...we are human. Today I
will not let my defects surface, I will bury them in
the past where they belong.
Today I will have faith, hope and compassion.
Where others may lie down.
I will get up and not just for me, but for
those who love me.
Forgive us our trespasses, because we all fall short.
Forgive me for I have trespassed also, I'm not
perfect, but I'm trying.

Great One,

Today, grant me pardon for my attitude. I laid asleep angry and awoke with guilt. I was under emotional attack, then responded with hurtful words.
Am I at fault because my marriage has little sustenance, my girlfriend uses me, I question my children's decisions and even worse, my own morals elude me. Oh Great One, I don't want to feel this way, I don't want to second guess my own code of conduct.
I laid asleep angry from fear. I was paralyzed by my own thoughts of being inadequate. Afraid to pray, for fear of what I may have prayed for, so I isolated.
Today, I will not make that mistake, I know our conversations end with great impact and serenity. I know there's power on my knees and power in my surrender.

Great One, remember my prayers, my vowels, my relationship, my kids and my life.

Amen

Learning to trust your decisions gives you power over circumstances
Committing to those decisions allows you to control your life
Actions cause progress
Progress defines who you will become

God of Abraham,

Today make me strong with will, creditable to my
friends and merciful to my enemy.
Help me walk in your light and not in the shadows, help
me proclaim my beliefs in your word, transmit your
love and wisdom to my mind, so my actions
reflect your orientation.
God, Heal all those who seek refuge in Worldly things,
give them a place in your kingdom and remove the mud
from their eyes.
Protect the innocent, fend for the weak and give
courage to those who call upon you today.
Give me the ability to walk in your glory so with each
step I take, I leave a beautiful footprint for
others to see.

Amen

Master of the Universe,

There has to be more depth to this life. Your kingdom seems so far, yet death appears close.
As I sit through this storm I realize how inadequate and meek my flesh truly is.
I cower at the thunderous sound of your voice, lighting demonstrates your power striking from heaven to earth.
Beneath me the earth trembles with wrath, not as punishment but as a reminder, a warning of human corrosion.
Master, at times we are sick, we need healing hands, I can admit first. It's me who needs mercy. Teach me today because my mind is clear, untainted, focused and unmolded.
Day after day we forage for money, lust and belongings like worker ants, but where is the truth, honor and loyalty.
Am I merely a machine, cold, programmed or emotionless.
Not me, no, not me.
Today, give me love, laughter and life.

Amen

I'm not destroyed...just broken.
I'm not impaired...just bruised.
I'm not departed...just lost and
though I am broken, I will mend.
My bruises will heal and
new life will be found.

TRUhope

My Lord,

I thank you for answering my prayers,
for yesterday and today.
I thank you for your benevolence, understanding
and sympathy for us who require it.
Today I stand with all my worldly possessions,
and I am grateful to understand my true proprietary.
My comfort is knowing that what I have surrounding
me and what I hold in my hands,
means nothing in comparison
to what I have in my heart.
Although material objects are comfortable.
Honesty, integrity and compassion give me solace
before I sleep tonight.
For this I thank you.

Amen

Teacher of all things,

Today, make me a faithful servant, help me sort through my troubles, anxieties and the non-sense. Direct my actions and emotions as I leave destructive formalities in the distance.
Grant me serenity, endurance and the will to keep moving forward in a positive manner.
Give me sustenance, make your words and teachings live in me, show me a path that leads to nourishment, not famine.
Teach me the lessons of defeat and success, destruction and restoration, because I cannot understand or appreciate one without the other.

Amen

The healing process hurts, no matter the relationship, addiction or internal wounds. Whether, your body is injured, your mind unraveled or your spirit broken...mending is painful, but through transformation you will become stronger, capable and independent. Only through determination can you overcome pain

Great Pastor,

Today, as I read and find a new understanding of
your Word, help me interpret and apply your
principles back into my life.
Help me gain perspective on the situations around
me that require attention.
I don't want to lose sight of who I am and
who I have become.
On this day, walk with me, allow me to shadow your
movements and realize my mistakes are part of
human life and without them I would have no story,
no view or no testimony.
Miserable failure come with glorious revival,
recovery and new life.
Thank you for transformation, for giving me a gift, a
voice and words that may aid more people to a
better cause, well being and
a better life.

Amen

Watcher of this place,

Today protect me, hold me... Anoint me.
I am not feebleminded, nor is the world around me,
but we all need direction.
If I am well, I will help, it's what you called me to do.
In your eyes we are a great establishment of people, but we
become weary and impatient.
With each day comes a greater cause and every step in time
reveals new challenges and consequences that we must
control and respond to, not just react.
As a responsible human being, I will love and
respect myself first.
You have taught me to love and respect everyone around me,
but it's difficult sometimes.
I must remind myself that I am only a messenger...
no more, no less.
I will not allow my moral judgment to be compromised by
dark influences.
I am a man of your cloth, the word and light.
Although sometimes I get lost.
Watcher, give me the ability to shine on those who need you
the most, the ones who seek you, practice your word, but also
live in your mercy.

Amen

It takes courage to say and do what you feel in your heart. Sometimes, your mind will battle for what it sees, but when your heart & mind argue... follow your heart.

My King,

I have forgotten my promise to you, I read your sacred words and abandoned them.
Please forgive me.
I have broken hearts, shattered friendships and pushed away those who love me.
If there is one thing I know in my heart, it's that you will not renounce me.
Are you a punishing ruler? No, you're fair and loving, and like my father before this time, I will always serve you.
I was weak in the moment, lonely, broken-hearted and afraid.
I kneel, I will make this right, my amends will touch many and I will overcome my old obsession and addictions.
I will gladly destroy repeated enslavement and live up to our agreement.
I promised to help others bury their past burdens, addictions and transgressions.
I am with you My King.
Grant me focus, fortitude and gratitude.

Amen

In this world we measure success by what we have and how much we have.
I want a car...a fast car
I need a house...with 8 bedrooms
I have 4 purses...Dolce & Gabbana
I need sunglasses...Marc Jacobs
I'm not a secretary...I'm a lawyer
I have money...I want to be rich
I shop...but only at the mall
I'll be beautiful with fake breasts
She'll love me...only with muscles
He'll love me... If I sleep with him
Please don't misunderstand this, we are all guilty of false security.
Success is not measured by what or how much you have. It is measured by who you are and what you have become.
Success seems to be a measurement, not living.
You are a person, not an object.
Share love, show kindness, pray for peace and live in gratitude.

There is no **FREEDOM** without surrender. Love what you do and who you are.

One of our greatest illusions is that we have control.
Our worst fear is that we do have control.
My delusion of satisfaction is that I have control.
My worst attributes is when I think I have control.
We mislead ourselves because we can't control.
We diminish our self-control .
We give up our morals, values and integrity because of
the thought of control .
We demoralize our bodies and minds because
we lose control.
We sacrifice our dreams for an illusion of control.

The TRUTH is we have no control; The only actual
control we have is the ability to control the way we
react to the fact that we don't have control.

Lord,

I am not perfect, no matter in who's eyes but yours alone do I admit this.
Sometimes this world and my emotions get to me, I'm human.
I am not flawless but lord I am no longer the failure I once was, I'm no longer that man of the past.
There's still pain, but not enough to debilitate me.
I'm much stronger, grounded and worthy. Not to the world lord, but to myself.
This place is not perfect, I'm not perfect, but the more I pray I see.
I see this place.

Amen

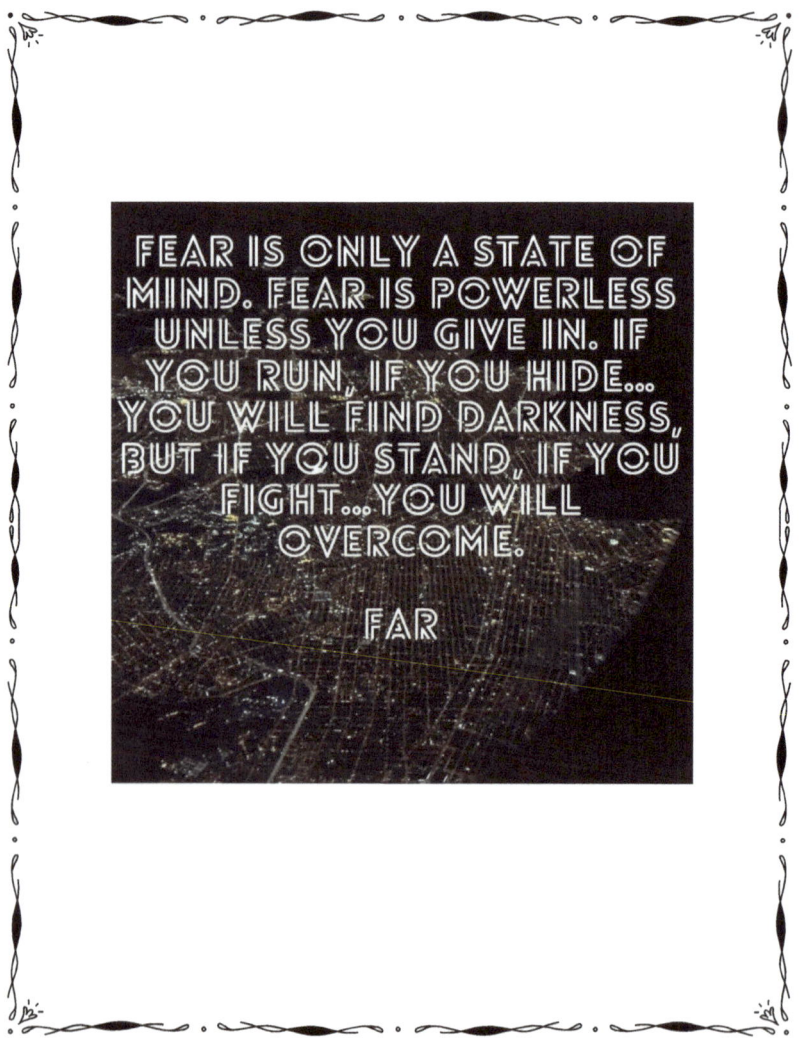

FEAR IS ONLY A STATE OF MIND. FEAR IS POWERLESS UNLESS YOU GIVE IN. IF YOU RUN, IF YOU HIDE... YOU WILL FIND DARKNESS, BUT IF YOU STAND, IF YOU FIGHT...YOU WILL OVERCOME.

FAR

Almighty,

Thank you for getting me through this weekend
without havoc, ruin or failure.
Thank you for guiding me through the storm, for
keeping me strong when I was weak, picking me
up when I fell and keeping me humble in the
face of my own pride.
Almighty, thank you for friends I can trust,
family I can love, and people who show me
unconditional signs of love.
Embrace me this week.
Make me unbreakable, resilient, yet humble.
Protect me from my own arrogance,
greed and lust.
Wash the mud from my eyes, so that I am not
blind to the world around me.
Help me see clearly.

Amen

Yeshua,

Today I ask for patience and reasoning. I don't
understand why I have to struggle,
why do I have hard times?
Why can't life be easy? Am I so bad? I have
problems with relationships, school, work,
money and insecurities.
Why me lord....why?
I think I'm a pretty good person.
why does my sickness not heal?
Why does my past drive me insane? Why do my
kids hate me? why do my friends ignore me?
I don't have the patience to understand.
Why doesn't the world think of me?
Why don't they know what I'm going through?
More importantly, why don't they care?
Is patience and understanding
gifts we already posses?
Is freedom just a trick? If not, where is it and
why don't I deserve it?
Are you listening to me or am I talking in the
wind? ....Talking to a ghost.
Oh great one, where are you?

Amen

Every *Dream* begins by believing in yourself. No one determines your *Success*, don't allow them to destroy your confidence in who you are. You have the *Power* to make your dreams materialize.

Please say this out loud...if you believe.

I am not a coward, nor am I afraid of challenges.
I can overcome any obstacle, including my past.
I will not allow your words to affect me,
nor will your hands lay upon me.
I will not allow your ignorance to
dictate my serenity.
I will not whisper the truth.
I will not react to negativity, but I will respond.
I will not lie down in shame or crawl in guilt.
I will stand up just for today,
in this present moment.
I know it's easy to look at other peoples faults
instead of our own, but change starts with you.
You cannot change anyone.
Only you.

I smile, because It's all that I have.

I am grateful, so I give what I can.

I am happy, cause I have peace.

I get tired, yet sometimes I rest.

I try so hard, yet sometimes I fail.

I forgive, so that I can love.

I love, because I can.

Change today
Forgive yesterday
Pray for tomorrow

Life is beautiful, but some times we are not.
She's pretty and you're ugly.
She's so skinny, yet you're fat.
He's got money and you're broke.
He works out, yet look how lazy you are.
She made it, but you never will.
She raises her family, yet you destroyed yours.
She has confidence, but where's yours?
She has lots of friends and you're always alone.
He saves lives, while you ruin them.
She shows real love and you always get used.
He has so much, yet you barely have enough.
Life is beautiful.
Why can't we see that when
we look in the mirror?
Be grateful for what you have and who you are.
You are invaluable, beautiful and caring.
You are confident, you have integrity and
your joy shows.
Your laughter rings loud and you're going to leave a
mark where ever you go.

Love,
Me

They say not to be a quitter.

I quit ...being angry for no reason.
I quit...feeling sad at the wrong times.
I quit...feeling guilty, it's not my fault.
I quit...feeling shameful, the past is over.
I quit...acting jealous, now I'm happy.
I quit...saying hurtful words, because I'm ok.
I quit...drinking till I pass out, it's no way to live.
I quit... Lying, I became truthful.
I quit...being unfaithful, because it hurts.
I quit...drugs, I learned to love me.
I quit...feeling lonely, now I have friends.
I quit...hating, so I love unconditionally.
I quit ...feeling sorry for myself,
my whole life changed.

What about you?
What have you quit ?

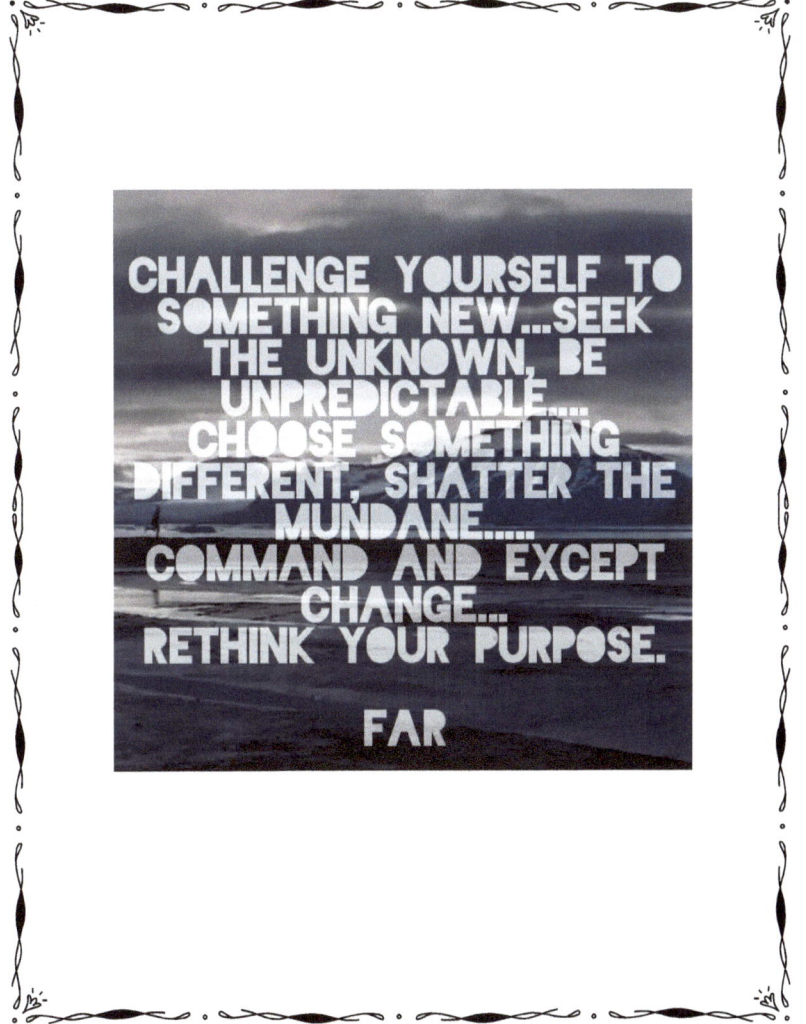

CHALLENGE YOURSELF TO SOMETHING NEW...SEEK THE UNKNOWN, BE UNPREDICTABLE....
CHOOSE SOMETHING DIFFERENT, SHATTER THE MUNDANE.....
COMMAND AND EXCEPT CHANGE...
RETHINK YOUR PURPOSE.

FAR

My God,

Thank you for yesterday.
Thank you for touching my heart, opening my eyes
and breaking my chains of self bondage. Concrete
walls were an obstacle, but selfishness is a dark
and lonely prison that secludes us from the
real joy of the world.
Greediness blinds us from real love,
we overlook the broken and forget our fellow man.
Why do I feel so trapped and alone,
confused and weary?
I know you shelter me, watch over me and
release me from self-bondage.
My ego is petty, it's weak but acts tough,
it's lonely yet shows fake smiles.
Help me Almighty, Give me the courage and
strength to fight my greatest enemy...
Me.

Amen

Spirit of the universe,

Today help me get over myself, help me seek
truth, help me to realize I am not alone.
I know sometimes I feel lost and alone, broken
and confused.
I know sometimes I can't forgive my enemy or
turn the other cheek, but I am only human.
Forgive me my insecurities, my trespasses and
all my doubts.
I don't want to live alone and afraid of my own
shadow, help me find strength to surrender my
ego and let down my guard, so I can be loved.
Smash these walls I cannot climb, strengthen
me, so I may conquer fears I don't understand.
Help me trust, forgive and have faith not only in
you, but in people too.

Amen

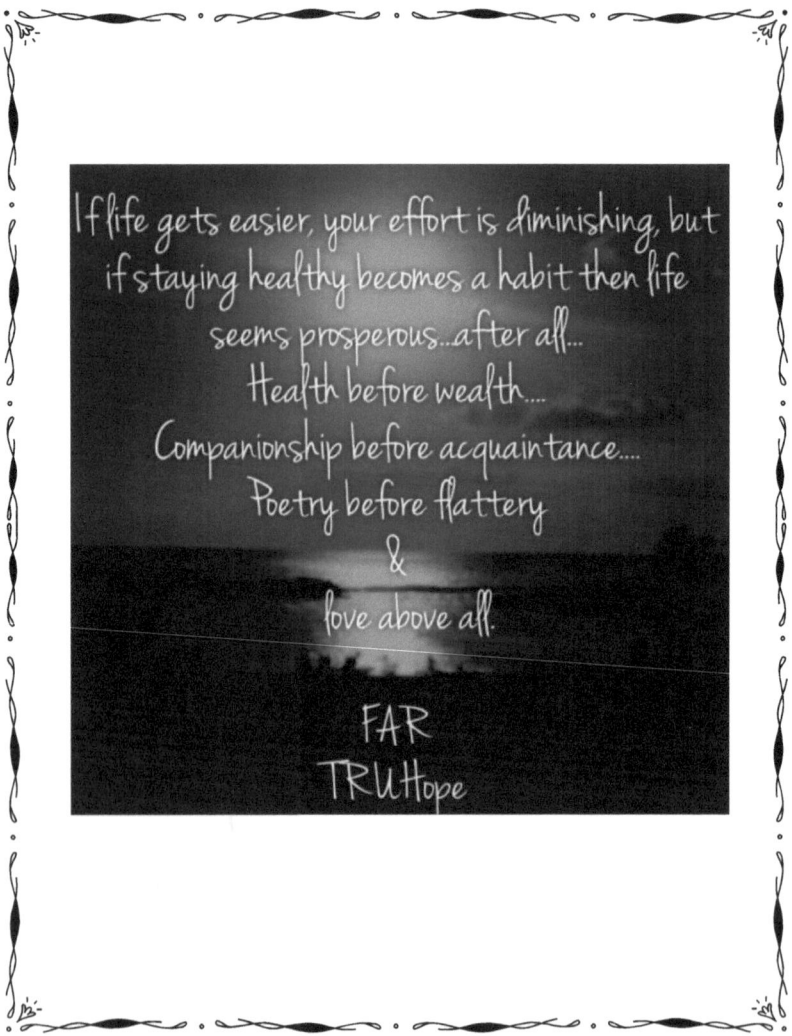

If life gets easier, your effort is diminishing, but if staying healthy becomes a habit then life seems prosperous...after all...
Health before wealth....
Companionship before acquaintance....
Poetry before flattery
&
love above all.

FAR
TRUHope

Dear Heartache,

I have some questions....Why does my heart break when I think about you?
Why can't I change your photo in my mind, When is your perfume going to
no longer linger?
When is your taste going to leave my lips? If I close my eyes, I can still see
your smile and hear you giggle. If I reach out, I still feel you.
The trees sway back and forth like we danced, they remind me of you.
I see your eyes at nightfall, they shine like stars in the sky.
Nothing mattered when we were together;
no past, no future, only now.
Time stood still.
When I held you the world stopped, my fears melted away.
you gave me hope and comfort. You gave me companionship.
Why would you leave me alone...broken, shattered, bruised and
completely lost?
Why can't you hold me, kiss me or make love to me? I'm crying alone.
You're not fair, why can't you love me? Am I too crazy?
LoVe is crazy, but beautiful, everlasting like your
half-smile in the morning,
like your peck on the cheek before you leave for work, like when you get
embarrassed in public because I'm dancing in the grocery isle.
Then you dance with me.
LoVe is genuinely romantic, painfully passionate, and funny....like when
you moved into your first apartment and had nothing but
boxes for a table,
with bathroom candles for date night.
LoVe's making love in the rain because you locked the keys in the car and
made the most of it.
It's laughing so hard that you spit wine all over the place, yes people stare
but its because they wish they were in-love like that.

Don't compare your LoVe with others,
share LoVe, show LoVe, embrace LoVe.......
Be LoVe.

Sometimes we can't change what we've said or done,
sometimes we can't live with what we've done and
sometimes we can't understand what we've done, but
through prayer and meditation
you will gain guidance, wisdom and strength.
You will know that your past doesn't define
who you are, but who you left behind.
When you have faith in your prayer and in your God,
you will no longer suffer
from the shame and guilt of the past.
Today choose the right path.
Today you create a new future.
Today I pray.

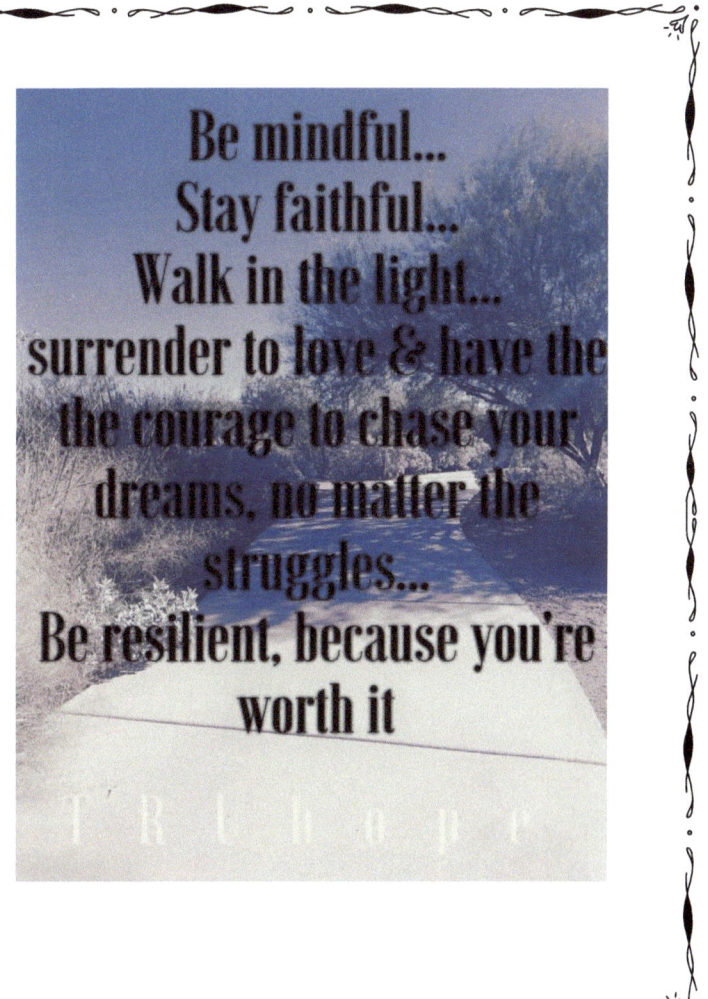

Be mindful...
Stay faithful...
Walk in the light...
surrender to love & have the
the courage to chase your
dreams, no matter the
struggles...
Be resilient, because you're
worth it

Lord,

Thank you for blessing me this day.
Today lord help me see things as they are,
help me notice the lost, needy and helpless.
Give me strength to do the right thing,
even when I don't want to.
Grant me compassion for the ignorant,
wisdom for the intolerable and
patience for the anxiety,
that today will certainly bring.
Keep me, embrace me and love me,
so that I may love me and with gratitude,
love others.

Amen

My King,

Don't let me lose sight of my dream today.
Make me relentless in my chase for hope.
Guard me as judgement nears, show my persecutors
love and tolerance,
let those who judge my conduct make soft decisions,
unless they themselves tread on water.
Give them understanding and
me acceptance.
Mistakes happen in life, but I do not regret them,
I learn from them. Gain experience for the next battle,
the next struggle.
Failing reminds me I'm human, it's evidence of inferiority,
it keeps me humble.
Failing is an action, a repercussion, it's not who I am or
who I've become. It's merely a consequence of lack of discipline,
maturity and patience.
Today I do not expect failure, I watch for the lesson
hidden in today's challenges.
I carefully analyze myself, my actions and my feelings, so I may
act carefully and appropriately.
My King, give me maturity with discipline and
everlasting patience.

Amen

Life has struggles, but it shouldn't always be a struggle. Let go of the guilt & shame in your heart, so you can move on, forgive yourself. Leave your old battles on the field & march forward...I remember my conflicts, but I don't carry them with me.
You don't have to either.
TRUhope

OUR COURAGE IS NOT FORGED BY BATTLES WE'VE WON, BUT BY THE BATTLES WE'VE *chosen*

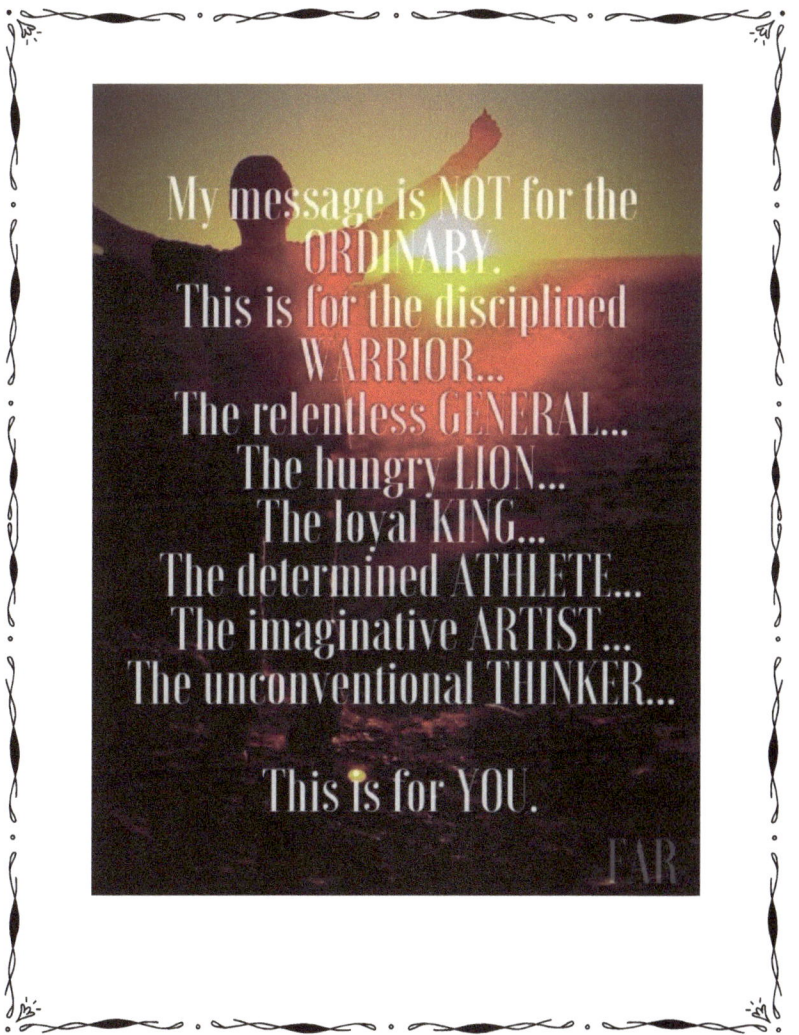

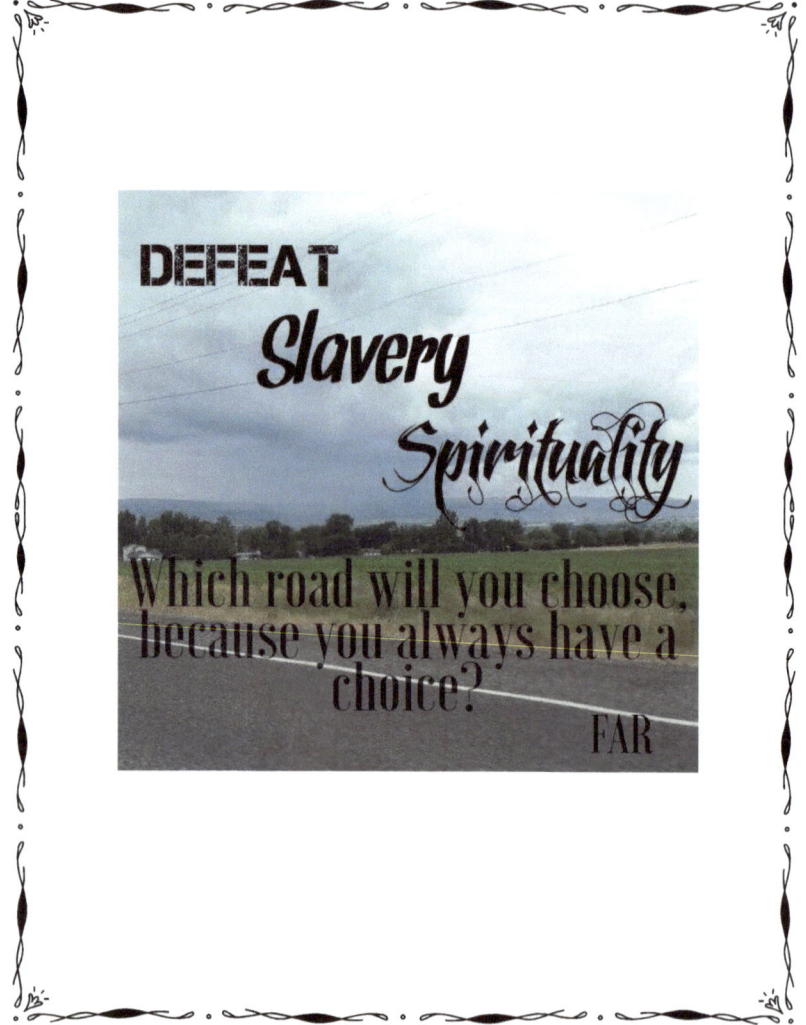

Lord,

I pray you grant me the power not to self-destruct,

but to have faith even when others have faded

Give me the courage to rise when I fall

Carve a path in my heart, where turmoil lies

I'm here...please find me when I'm lost

Amen

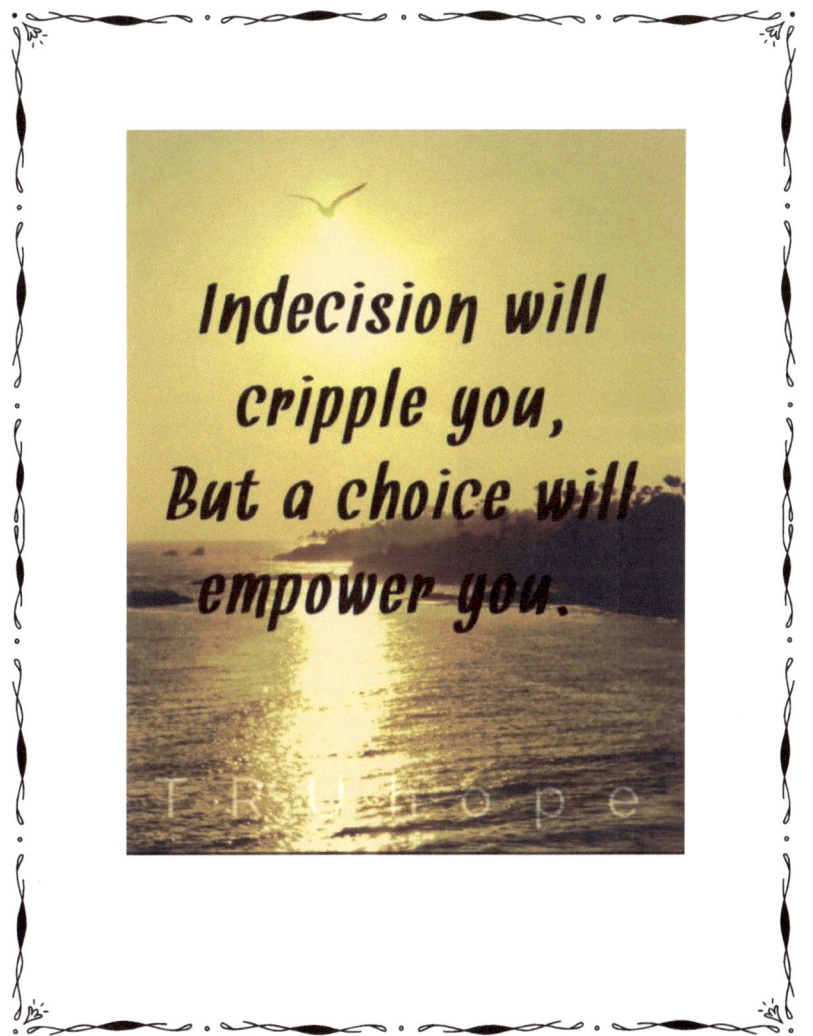

Indecision will cripple you, But a choice will empower you.

In the beginning of this book I told you I would finish my story about prison. Well, I showed up to prison like everyone one else who knows they just got caught, pissed off and slightly scared. For me, I had already been a part of the legal system for a while, but I hadn't been locked up for that long before, so I had plenty of time to get my life together. Of course this didn't happen in the beginning, I was the same selfish a-hole I was as before. I used and traded drugs in prison, just like I did on the streets. I gambled, fought and worked out just like in the movies, a real badass, so I thought. Only thing is, movies are fake and only last an hour or two.

My life was getting real sad and lonely for much longer than an hour. I began missing little things at first, like fresh fruits and vegetables', privacy and girls, then I started missing my family and friends(who didn't like me much, because I was a terror), I just missed going outside to see the sun or rain when I wanted. I wanted to go to work without a guard stripping me down and looking where other people normally don't look when you leave a kitchen(and yes, you know what I'm getting at, if you've seen any prison movies)! Anyways, after a few years I just got tired, people around me and outside of prison were dying, and I was watching life come and go with no purpose or meaning behind it. I was living life through mail and 15 minute phone call. My baby girl who I had just had right before I went in was mumbling her first words, taking her first steps and having her 4th birthday party without me. I was a ghost, a shell of a man, some picture of a man who once had all these loving things surrounding him, but blew it. I needed to change, I had all this knowledge of how to change, but what I didn't have was discipline, I mean of course I didn't have discipline, I was living in a cell with three boxes(which held all my possessions for life) and a see-through T.V.. There is this famous saying, perhaps you've heard it "Don't talk about it, be about it!"

After a year I came across this podcast ran by Swami Tyagananda, who was a Vedanta teacher from Harvard's religious studies. I heard him talk about discipline and self-Inquiry to understand your purpose in life and I was hooked. I followed his study courses everyday for 3 years, twice a day most days and something began to change in me that even I didn't understand. I knew from then on that my life was going to change, I didn't know how or when but for the first time in my life, I would learn discipline.

Everyday I practice a meditation technique called "Atma-Vichara", which is a Sanskrit word that means "self-inquiry". This form of meditation causes one to look within, to find the true meaning of your life. It asks profound questions; such as why am I here? What is my purpose and who am I? Yes, these are deep questions, but for me they were questions that I was forced to ask myself because I was heading down a road that only lead to misery. Isn't this similar for some of us, we feel alone in a dark place, stuck in an emotional or physical prison, just waiting for a "come to Jesus", or self reflective moment to save us.

In the midst of sitting quietly and searching for me, I found myself reading more, learning and studying different philosophers, ancient wisdom books, such as the bible, the dhammapada, the upanishads and any other literature on spiritual wisdom or meditation. I loved this book called the Bhagavad Gita. I don't know why, but you'll have to read it to gain your own experience. Everything I read had an impact on me, all these scriptures showed me something, that suffering wasn't unique to me. Many of us have been suffering for many years, I learned it's a part of human nature. There is pain and loss, but there's also joy and beauty everywhere we look. I learned that my suffering was coming from within me. I thought it was from my external conditions, but I was very wrong. You see, it wasn't because I was doing the wrong things, it was because of the way I was thinking and feeling. Where there is action, there is reaction, cause and effect or karma if you think in these terms.

Let me give you an example; when I was young, I was taken advantage of, there was lots of pain, anger and confusion that came with this tragic event. So, this event was the action, I suffered dearly for many years loathing, drinking, drugging and living like a fool. This was my reaction, it worked some times, but long term this was not a solution. While I sat in my cell sitting with this thought/event in my life, self-inquiry meditation helped me understand this event was in the past, I wasn't really suffering now. In my mind I kept bringing up this event and causing myself more hurt because I wasn't looking at the actual solution. I kept blaming this past event for how I was feeling right now, in the present moment. I was blinded by blame, and ignorance of not knowing how to manage my emotions. I kept using it to fuel my feelings, which didn't make sense anymore. I'll put this in simple terms, "I was hurting myself now, because of something that happened when I was a kid. I know what your thinking, you didn't hurt yourself, someone else did this to you! You're right and you're wrong. This is why. Blaming an external circumstance for how I feel, is wrong. See blaming doesn't allow you to take responsibility for your reactions. Past events are over, you cannot change them, I had to look at myself and take responsibility for what and how I was reacting to this emotional trigger. I could change this reaction, and I did. I sat with it in meditation and said " I'm going to forgive this tragedy, and not only that, but I'm going to forgive myself for all the blame, shame and guilt I lived through regarding this event".

I decided I wasn't a victim anymore, victims use blame so they don't have to take responsibly for themselves, emotions or reactions. Trust me this was hard, this realization hurt, but the truth is that beyond pain and truth there's freedom. There is great freedom when you find out that you have the power to choose who you are. Playing that victim kept me a prisoner in an endless cycle of anger, shame, blame and guilt.

In the beginning of this book I also told you I would teach you how to take your life back, here it is.

I'll tell you and then give a small reason on how this works. I want you to understand something though, If you quit this before 90 days or only practice here and there, it won't work. Changing a habit or lifestyle takes discipline without it change will be nearly impossible. I tell my clients this, imagine you're trying to cross the ocean in a row boat. If you paddle one ore at a time, will you get across the ocean, sure, but it may take a lifetime or two. Now, If you use both paddles in sync you will get there much quicker. It's your choice, this boat is you and your sufferings are the ocean. How long do you want to be stuck out there?

First thing we do to change is.... take responsibility for your thoughts, emotions, actions and reactions. Instead of blaming and playing a victim. Learn something new like Reading books to help you keep your mind stimulated, play an instrument, Garden, hike, exercise, learn to draw or write in a journal, so you have an outlet for your feelings. Talk to a counselor, friend or family member you trust. Do anything that keeps you focused on the now.

This brings me to the second thing; Stay present, dwelling in the past and losing yourself in anxiety about the future does absolutely nothing for change. This is actually very simple, so don't complicate it. When you're learning something new or engaging with someone or an activity, focus on that person or thing. Don't judge or have an opinion about everything, of course you're human and we all do this but do it and then move along. When you judge and have too many opinions on something. You tend to go to the past or future very quickly, because you need all these old or upcoming concepts to support all this drama. So, leave it alone. Don't overthink this, honestly when you're learning something new you're already pretty present.

The third thing is meditation. I know what your thinking, "I can't sit still and quiet my mind"! Meditation is actually something many of us do but aren't aware of it. When you're running or driving and you lose time and all of a sudden you snap back into reality. You just meditated, unaware of it. Meditation is just bringing your focus to one point, such as one sound, feeling or other sensation.

You could call it absolute concentration, of course there is many ways to practice a meditation. For this, I just want you to take 5 minutes in the morning and sit with headphones on, listen to nature sounds or soft piano music, anything to just block out the noise of your house for the moment. Just sit, have your favorite tea or coffee, close your eyes, smell the aroma of the coffee, feel the hot steam rolling through your nostrils and just breath naturally, just notice your breathing and soft sounds, they're just relaxing you nothing more. If you already practice a meditation or use an app, just use that. Do this everyday, don't skip days. Remember the story of the row boat. Keep this in mind, meditation allows you to get in touch with you, If your mind brings up emotions or old concepts you don't like, don't quit, look at why those things are coming up. Sit with your emotions, cry or get mad if you need to, but when the 5 minutes or longer is over, be done with it. This is what helps you take responsibility for you, going through this helps you discover what new thing to learn, you see these three things I'm telling you are tied together, which leads me to the fourth thing.

Forgiveness. I'm going to tell you something that you may not like or understand, and it's not because you don't know this, it's because many of us don't experience this. Remember my tragic life event I told you about, well for many years I said "I forgive my perpetrator, I don't want that person to have that power over me", at-least that's what I said, because my therapist or counselor told me to do some forgiveness exercises. They were on the right track, but hear this. Forgiveness is not a word, we don't forgive someone or something. We forgive ourselves, for being a victim unknowingly. Now you see how change can be made. Forgiveness is in the action you live by. I forgave myself for everything I had done because I needed it right then, not in the past, we can't go backwards or forward, you only ever live right now. So, forgive yourself and do these four things so you can live free now, not later.

The last thing I'll tell you, these four steps will develop in time, they may evolve into something great or help you leave your addictions(bad habits) and traumas behind, but above all it will help you discover who you are. Personally, my meditation practice helped me discover that God was not outside of me, but really, my peace, my God....everything was inside of me. I cannot explain this any simpler than this. I hope this book touched your heart as it did mine. Looking back at all these writings gave me hope and showed me you can do this, please understand that no matter the addiction, heartache, trauma, past or suffering; there is a way to soothe your pain and live joyful. This process is within you, it's within all of us, it just takes some practice.

Namaste

I want to thank everyone who stood by me
through high tides and low,
who cried as much as I did and
now who can laugh about it.

I love you

Nowadays, I am a certified Substance abuse counselor and author who works in the behavioral health field and teaches meditation on the weekends. I live in Arizona and teach online courses on emotional wellness when I am not helping out the community or spending time with my family. I am a student of Swami Sarvadevananda of the Rama-Krishna order and through his teachings my practice is action through experience, my words mean nothing if I cannot show you that a better way of living is possible.

Namaste

WWW.TRUhope.Blog

www.ingramcontent.com/pod-product-compliance
Lightning Source LLC
Chambersburg PA
CBHW040847120626
46547CB00001B/58